The Grandfather Thing

By Saul Turteltaub

[with the real poop by Max, age one]

TallfellowPress

Published by
Tallfellow Press, Inc.
1180 S. Beverly Drive
Los Angeles, CA 90035

Cover and interior design by Rick Penn-Kraus

ISBN 0-9676061-6-0

Printed in China

10   9   8   7   6   5   4   3   2

To
Mommy, Daddy, Bubbe, MomMom and PopPop

Love,
The Authors

My publishers, Larry Sloan and Leonard Stern, saw a book in this material when I thought it was just something to copy and send to my family as presents and thereby save a lot of money.

My editor and friend, Bob Lovka, is as good a writer as I am and was willing to help me with my book when it would never enter my mind to help him with his.

I am tremendously grateful to Laura Stern and Claudia Sloan for their limitless amount of patience and kindness. They continue to solve all my computer related problems, most of them only minutes after they have shown me how to solve them myself.

Without Shirley Turteltaub, there would be no Adam Turteltaub and therefore no Max Turteltaub and therefore no book.

Table of Contents

Introduction

[Getting Ready]

So you're a grandfather. Congratulations. And don't attempt the glib response, "Hey, I had nothing to do with it." You had a lot to do with it. You raised one of its parents, gave up a lot of time, love and money to do so, and now that person you raised is staring at his or her new child thinking, "Don't worry, sweetheart, I won't make all the mistakes my parents made with me."

Your children from this day on will treat you as if you are a complete idiot, starting with giving you instructions on holding the baby, like, "Be careful," "Support its head" and "Don't fool around." Of course you will want your son or daughter to be the most loving and caring parent possible so don't defend yourself; allow them their unreasonable concern. Simply wait until they are looking away and then quickly be careless and fool around.

The most important thing to realize when the baby is born is that you are not gaining a grandchild, you are losing a wife. If you ever thought you would always be the most important person in the world to her, you will learn that is not true. Her grandchild now has that title. She will think about the baby all the time, and will be with it every minute possible. If it is a boy, she will occasionally call you by its name. She will show it more love and worry than you will remember her showing her own children, probably because she thinks this baby is underprivileged, not having her for its mother.

You will also love your grandchild (eventually) but never with the same intensity as your wife does, which is good because there should be one sane person in every household.

It is important to publish your position paper early, so when you refuse to change diapers later it will not be taken personally. I got off that hook immediately by telling my son and daughter-in-law that my idea of changing the baby is taking him to an orphanage and coming home with one that's toilet trained. Fortunately, no one expects grandfathers to do any of the dirty work, so don't screw it up for the next guy. Go see the baby as often as you like and as often as you are allowed and walk away from anything about the kid that bothers you, i.e., crying, smells and facial food. Everyone else involved will chuckle at you and no one will think you should do more. When the child gets older, you might be expected to come through with financial aid, like tuition assistance and money toward a house. That will be up to you, but remember, if you live long enough to be needed to help the grandchild buy a house, you will probably be close to needing that grandchild to visit you, help you up and wheel you to a mall.

If it matters to you what your grandchild will call you, think of that name right away because this generation of parents asks you what you want their child to call you. If you really want to be called "Grampa," declare that immediately or you may be stuck with something you will later regret, like "Gampie," "Poppy" or as two grandfathers I know with German backgrounds, "Fahtie."

Don't be ashamed that you are less mechanical than your daughter or daughter-in-law. She will quickly learn by instruction and experience how to assemble and disassemble the high chair, car seat and stroller. Stay out of it. Don't volunteer to do it. You will get mad, look silly and possibly end up in an emergency room. If you are sensitive about these things, don't buy your grandchild any toy that needs assembling unless you spend several hours at home assembling it first. Also, do not leave any toy store until you are shown the batteries that are supposed to come with the battery-operated toy. You will also be doing yourself a favor by asking the salesperson to install them. Always remember, being the grandfather means having the most fun and bearing the least responsibility of all the relatives of the baby, and you'll see, by not bothering them about their dirty underwear, and scraping the food off their face with a spoon, you'll be the one they love the most.

Max
at One
Month

[What Really Matters]

y prayers for a healthy baby born to a healthy mother were answered. How many times did I say to God and my family and friends, "All that matters is that the child and the mother are healthy." But I was not honest. I soon learned their health was not all that mattered, and my only defense, meager as it may be, is I didn't realize it until yesterday, when I saw my grandson again, one month after he was born: it also matters to me that he looks like the other grandfather. It matters to me a lot. I hate it.

I don't blame either one of them and I certainly don't blame God, although I do believe He could have made the baby look like me if He wanted to, but why should He want to? I didn't ask Him. Who ever thinks to ask, "If it's a boy, don't let him look like the other grandfather?" Not that the guy is so terrible to look at. He has what my wife calls "a nice face." It's a round face, rather than classically elongated as mine is. But that has nothing to do with it. I'm thinking of the baby.

Generally it seems wrong for a grandson to look like one grandfather and not the other. People will think, for no reason at all, that the grandfather he looks like is closer to him and that he loves that grandfather more. That is stupid!

Clearly our grandson should not have looked like either grandfather. He should have looked like his father, just as his father looks exactly like me.

Max Observes:

- Don't assume that just because I look like somebody, that person is more important than somebody else.
- I don't need anything from you yet so make the fuss over my parents. They are my full-time caretakers and I want them to think they are wonderful so they'll do a good job.

- Please don't buy me anything that will make me look stupid when I grow into it.
- Don't talk to me. We both know I can't understand or respond. I can only lose respect for you.
- Be patient! I'll grow up in five months.
- When you make that joke that you think is so cute about marrying me off to some other baby, please make sure the parents you are talking to are not from some country where that kind of talk is taken seriously.

Max's First Poem

Happy Birthday? Not a chance.
What kind of day is that?
Evicted with no shirt or pants
From a nice warm water flat.
Lights and faces wearing masks.
A terrorist attack!
I wish, if anybody asks,
My mommy'd put me back.

Max
at Two
Months

[The Grandfather Thing]

Regarding my two-month-old grandson, Max, I do not have "The Grandfather Thing," and do not feel guilty about it.

"The Grandfather Thing," by common definition, is believing that the newborn grandchild is the most beautiful creation in the world, although any souvenir cushion is more attractive. It's wanting to see the baby any hour of the day and wanting to hold it and kiss it and believing it likes you doing that. It's taking dozens of pictures of it and showing them to strangers in the next car at a traffic light.

I am not surprised that I don't have "The Grandfather Thing." I didn't have those reactions to my own children, one of whom is Max's father, until they were five or six months old, really cute, and made it crystal clear that they thought I was wonderful. I do take a lot of pictures of Max, but that is because I am the designated picture taker of the family. I have walked backwards across Europe taking pictures of my family walking frontwards.

In truth, to anyone other than his parents or his grandmother, he is not an awful lot of fun to be around. While he is no uglier than any other two-month-old baby, he is no prettier. People of that age are not pretty, and as unattractive as they are at rest, they are even more so when awake, making weird faces and looking God-knows-where at God-knows-what with half-closed eyes which God knows are not always in sync.

When he is not eating or sleeping, he is crying. He stops only for a few minutes when carried, bounced or patted into a new position. It seems totally irrational that his parents and grandmother – who only get trouble from him – are totally in love with him; and he who gets nothing but patience, love and understanding from them seemingly barely tolerates them.

I am told things will change, that the time will come when I will look forward to visits with him and happily play with him and revel in his laughter. I give him four more months or he will go to a state college if he's counting on help from me.

Max Observes:

- I don't like my crying either but at this point it's all I have. (And you have to admit it works.)

- I don't know what you think you saw, but that was not a smile. I don't do smile yet.

- Don't you ever wonder why I like my bath so much? It's the only good memory I have of the good old days in Mommy's tummy. Nice warm water and that weird hose attached to my stomach.

- I like watching toys that turn to music, but don't expect that to keep me quiet all day. Change the tune or the toy once in awhile.

- I don't know one single kid that likes Brahms' Lullaby.

Max's Second Poem

I'm just two months but not a fool,
So keep your pacifier.
The look and taste is not the same
The inside is much drier.
So pass the breast and save the con,
I'm not fooled for a minute.
The nipple doesn't turn me on
It's all the goodies in it.

Max
at Three
Months

[Becoming Somebody]

I have learned firsthand that it takes a grand-son three-and-a-half months to lose his unattractiveness. Max at this point in his life is not unattractive. This does not mean he has arrived at "cute," only that he no longer looks wrinkled and newbornlike. All the praise, flattery and cooing he receives from loving family and insincere friends still is clearly something they emit for personal reasons rather than something he truly deserves.

He still does nothing that indicates any creativity or purpose. He smiles, but never at the right time, and no grandfather in his right mind is fooled into thinking he is smiling in response to something that grandfather *did*. Proof? He does not smile when poked in the ribs with a finger or when the grandfather blows trumpet-style through clenched lips directly onto his stomach.

He smiles when looking at the ceiling. The plain, white, unfunny ceiling.

The good news at this point is he can exhibit readily that all his senses function:
• When he hears someone talking, he cries.
• When he sees someone talking, he cries.
• And when he feels someone poking him in the ribs or blowing into his stomach, he cries.

But he has an acceptable face when smiling at the ceiling.

Max Observes:

● Just because I don't smile doesn't mean I don't like what you're doing. I'll cry when it bothers me.

● Since I spend most of my time lying on my back, it really seems strange that you have pictures on the walls and not on the ceilings. It makes me laugh every time I think about it!

● None of us likes the passing around from person to person thing. I know most of those people gave us presents, but hey, they're not going to ask for them back, right?

Max's Third Poem

At two months old I liked to eat,
And sleep and poop and pee,
Now add to that my stroller,
And the car and loud tv.
I recognize my mom and dad,
And like their smiling faces.
I don't know why they like to rub
   their nose in all my places.
I guess I'm finally growing up;
In two weeks I'll be four.
They'll expect a lot of stuff from me
Like smiles and laughs and more.
I'll give them everything I've got
And even try to talk,
But I love it when they carry me,
So they'll wait to see me walk.

Max
at Four
Months

[The Smile and the Grasp]

So Max and I ended up at the same wedding in New York this past weekend. His parents and grandmother were anxious to show him off to the rest of the family. Personally, I would have waited until it was *his* wedding when there would be more to show off. His only new accomplishment at four-and-a-half months is that he smiles and he grasps. He smiles at a lot of physical comedy. He doesn't seem to be into the cerebral stuff yet. Holding his feet against my cheeks and kissing his ankles alternately while making a sound similar to "yummmyyumbumm-bumymyumy" works regularly, as does sticking my tongue out and squeaking. (As you can see, I am trying hard to get "The Grandfather Thing" which, if it finally comes, I know will endear me to the rest of my family. However, I refuse to fake it, only because I imagine if I finally get it, it will be much different from what I would fake and they will all know I was faking.) Saying "I beg your pardon!" and feigning great offense when he burps does not yet work, although his mother and four-year-old cousin Jake laughed. (It is apparently a sign of the times that children are given names of very old people. Max and Jake's two other male cousins are Nathan and Sam. They all seem destined to open a Ghetto.) Max did insure his financial security, however, by smiling once at the sight of me. I would have been more impressed if it were not the same smile he gives to the ceiling.

As for the grasping, my wife ("Bubbe," she chose to be called) brought him a stuffed toy, and he actually reached for it and grasped it, which excited many people who are apparently easy to excite. As a historic note, at four-and-a-half months he is now on solid food. Actually, the solid food is on *him* as he rejects each spoonful. Perhaps this is part of the reason he has not yet captivated me. To be captivated, I think I, and anyone else more into intelligence than emotion, need to hear some actual words from him, like, but not necessarily, "I love you, Grampa."

Max Observes:

- If you're trying to feed me solid food, get some that tastes good; and when you're ready to feed me, tell me to open my mouth. I have no idea what a garage door is.

- I don't sleep through the night sometimes because I'm not exhausted. What have I done all day? Laid around, eaten and slept. When I'm old enough to drag myself around to toys that are interesting enough to keep me up, I'll sleep at night. In the meantime, try putting on the video of Great Car Crashes.

- What are "cousins" and how come I have so many of them? And if they're mine, why did we leave them in New York?

- About this traveling stuff: Why would anyone who loves me think I would like it? The car seat is uncomfortable in a car, let alone on a plane, or in a New York taxicab where the driver's face makes it very clear he doesn't want to take me anywhere. He'd probably like me better if he knew I didn't want to go.

- If you want to tell me when I'm ten that you took me to a baseball game when I was only four months old, tell me, don't take me. Who'll know? It's scary. People jumping up and shouting, bags of peanuts whizzing by. It's childish.

Max's Fourth Poem

Solid food is just a waste,
Isn't solid, has no taste.
I spit it out and so would you,
Why not a sugar cube or two?
Why not some soup like Bubbe makes?
Why not some pureed sirloin steaks?
And if you really want to thrill me,
A little Rocky Road won't kill me.

Max
at Five
Months

[Trying to Impress]

Well, the little guy is trying hard to beat his six-month deadline. According to his grandmother, he's beginning to show signs of cute at five-and-a-half months, at least in the way kids are cute at five-and-a-half months. While he's not the type of kid who needs you to blow into his stomach and make foolish sounds to give you a smile, he does smile at funny faces from distances up to ten feet. He's also apparently trying to impress me with his strength. When I hold him, I can feel him trying to stand up. He sits up on his own now which knocks his grandmother out; and she is not deflated when I point out he falls over in less than ten seconds. I honestly believe the wild admiration and respect he receives from her for questionable or minor accomplishments can only hurt him later in life. It would probably help him establish a greater system of values to observe his grandmother and parents lavishing properly deserved attention on his grandfather. On the plus side, the vacant stare is diminishing and he is actually swallowing his solid food now and showing some discrimination in his likes and dislikes. While he rejects oatmeal totally, he shows a liking for the feel of strained and pureed carrots in the jar, and will swallow half a spoonful on occasion.

I am told by his grandmother that his motor skills are through the roof. I honestly don't see it, but I have noticed that while almost standing in his round canvas walker he has learned to deal with all the challenging puzzles attached to its rim. I have to admit I was somewhat intrigued watching him sliding the rings over the arch and moving them back in the reverse direction with his other hand, possibly indicating he is ambidextrous. He spins the various wheels so casually it looks as if he was born to do it, and he slaps and pushes the blue shapeless figure with conviction as if to say, "I don't know what you are but I'm not afraid of you." Before I get too carried away with any talents this may show, I must question the manufacturer who possibly mislabeled the age qualifications on these toys only to make parents and grandparents feel good.

His crying now is decreased and specific, whereas it used to be often and random, in that sometimes the cause was clear, and other times there was no reason for it other than he was just acting like a baby. He seems to use his crying purposely now to indicate a frustration with his parents' failure to anticipate his needs.

Max Observes:

- Now that you know that if you sit me up I'll stay there a few seconds, stop it. I don't like falling down. When I really want to sit up I will do it myself.
- Getting me to laugh by tickling me is too easy. Let's hear a clever remark once in awhile.
- Thank you, Mommy and Daddy, for changing me when I'm wet and dirty. It is a little embarrassing. I can't wait until I'm old enough to change myself.
- I'm crazy about my feet, but something really worries me. Are my toes supposed to be as long as my fingers?

Max's Fifth Poem

I notice when I laugh and smile
My parents do it too,
But when I cry they only sigh
And don't know what to do.
"He's tired, hungry, or he's wet,"
Are all the choices that I get.
I'm five months old,
Why don't they guess,
"Perhaps he wants a game of chess."

Max
at Six
Months

[That Special Smile]

Last Wednesday night at my totally irregular poker game (the last one was a year ago), someone brought out a picture of his three-year-old grandchild as if the rest of us were interested. Surprisingly, the rest of them *were* interested in that it gave them an opportunity to show pictures of their grandchildren. After the reasonable amount of time for artificial complimenting, they turned to me and asked if I had a picture of Max. I conceded I had one but it was not just Max, it was a picture of Shirley, my wife, smiling beautifully holding Max. They insisted I fish it out and pass it around. I expected the "Hey, he's really cutes," but what surprised me completely was the repeated comment that he resembled me, that he was so mature looking, and that he had *my smile!* Until I heard the smile reference I was sure I accidentally had given them my driver's license. I took the picture back, studied it, and for the first time did see a slight resemblance. I admit I didn't recognize "my smile." I have no idea what "my smile" is, never having watched me smile. The resemblance I recognized was more in the attitude than the smile. He looked like he had my attitude! Like he was as nonchalant at having his picture taken as I was taking it. I like that in a baby. But as I now consider it, I find the thing about Max that's special at six months, in fact, is his smile. It's not too wide like some kids his age have which looks like someone jammed a banana in their mouth sideways, or too small that looks like some kind of studied rich baby smile, or a wide open-mouthed smile that indicates potential stupidity, but a well-shaped smile where the upper lip and lower lip are separated from the center symmetrically and the increased width is obvious but unstrained. As much as this sounds like the ranting of someone with "The Grandfather Thing," it is not. It is a simple factual description of a perfect smile! Max's use of his smile is exceptional. He neither throws it around indiscriminately at all people or all situations, nor does he withhold it, snoblike, from strangers. He smiles at someone who smiles at him if they look sincere. He smiles at family whom he has come to recognize, if they smile at him, and often if they don't. He smiles sometimes through tears if something strikes him funny, indicating a strong sense of values. Most importantly he smiles at "shtick," i.e., funny faces, a parent or grandparent hitting himself on the head with a toy, hitting him playfully with a harmless cloth kangaroo or playing advanced peekaboo hiding either your face or his face momentarily. It strikes me that Max has become cuter than most children, not only his age but of any age. Even children of another time, including Shirley Temple and Spanky of the Our Gang comedies. What's so wonderful about this is his lack of precociousness. He doesn't flaunt his cuteness or trade on it. He also has displayed an amazing sophistication in his eating habits. While still turning down pureed vegetables, he eats bits of bagel, a much harder food to swallow and digest but clearly more attractive and tasty. I see no reason why he shouldn't just soar into his seventh month well ahead of his contemporaries. Frankly, I believe he could skip the seventh month.

Max Observes:

- How about a voice-activated TV in my room that goes on at night when I cry? I like Lucy.
- Remind Daddy how tall he is. If he drops me during that airplane trick, it's curtains.
- Bring that Grampa guy around more. He knocks me out.

Max's Sixth Poem

It's not the food, I hate the seat,
It makes it take too long to eat.
No matter if I like the taste,
I haven't got the time to waste.
So much to learn, so much to know,
Why can't I have my meals to go?

Max
at Seven
Months

[Becoming Established]

Well, I've learned something about infants. At seven months old they are just about finished becoming established. Max's personality for the rest of his life is perfectly clear. He has a high intelligence that will not diminish. He focuses on what is important, i.e., his food, his family, his fingers, and dismisses things that do not matter, such as neatness. He has a finely tuned sense of humor. He laughs easily and unashamedly at things that are funny. I refer specifically to Bubbe squeezing Grampa's nose and Grampa responding with the sounds "Beep Beep." He is warm and receptive, smiling at all who approach him, putting them at ease and encouraging their friendship. He has a mature patience, sitting quietly by himself while his babysitting grandparents are preparing his or their dinner. He sits erect and well-balanced, and stands with only minimal support. He obviously does not yet say words familiar to grown-ups but he clearly is speaking in both mono- and polysyllabic sounds.

He is also kind and gentle. While he can be rough pulling eyeglasses off his grandmother's face, he never attempts to do so to her eyes, nose or ears. He has started growing teeth and with little objection. He has an acceptance of the inevitable. As he "teethes," he does so with very little whining. As far as his sleeping habits go, he is beginning to sleep through most of the night, and he is also eating his solid food willingly. All that remains now is for him to walk and talk in grown-up. This he will obviously accomplish weeks before his contemporaries, although the goodness that he appears to have will not allow him to gloat.

I am pleased that I was able to be objective in the early months. Neither Max nor I respect hypocrisy. A child at any age knows there is no reason for any adult to be thrilled that he or she sneezed all by himself. I am sure I can speak for him on this, as at seven months his mind is uncluttered and can easily detect uncalled-for flattery, unreasonable praise and tactfully displayed honesty. I sincerely believe that my pure objectivity played a huge part in making him the magnificent soul he is today!

Max Observes:

- Why does Grampa go "Beep Beep," when Bubbe squeezes his nose, and why does Bubbe squeeze his nose?
- If you're not going to give me the good food, don't eat it in front of me.
- Just a question: If breast milk is naturally kept at 98.6 degrees, how come when you put it in a bottle for me you have to refrigerate it?

Max's Seventh Poem

Seven was great,
I can't wait to be eight.
I think that's the month,
I can sleep on my fronth.

Max
at Eight
Months

[Clapping]

All right, so maybe I caught a touch of "The Grandfather Thing" and was too quick to report Max's progress. Quite bluntly, he does not sleep through the night and does not easily accept solid food. I am not accusing him of not liking or wanting solid food. The fact is he eats it from his parents' fingers. Not all of it, of course, since it is obviously difficult to pick up pureed carrots in one's fingers, but he happily eats all the bits of bread, meat and Cheerios he's hand-fed. The conclusion his parents have arrived at is he simply does not want to eat from a spoon. Now before everyone leaps up and shouts, "Ha, ha, so he's not such a genius after all," consider this: what he is doing is making a statement we should all subscribe to. He does not believe he or any of us should give up any direct human contact if it is not necessary. We should hold onto the intimacy of one another rather than insert the go-between of a cold and lifeless spoon. If only all children thought that way!

At eight months he showed his first clear sign of understanding the English language and the meaning of its words. He claps on demand. When told to "clap hands," he claps his hands (and never less than three times in a row). He also taught himself how to extricate his hands from each other when they got locked together following a clap. And, as a demonstration of his in-depth comprehension of the clapping chain (since following his response of clapping when told to do so his parents and all onlookers always shout, "Yayyy"), he will clap without the clap command whenever he hears someone shout, "Yayyy." What a kid!

Max continues to enjoy his bath and he demonstrates the most joy when being rubbed with oils and powders on his dressing table following his bath. At only the age of eight months, he plays Peekaboo BY HIMSELF. He repeatedly raises a towel over his face and suddenly lowers it, revealing a big smile with or without the question, "Where's Max?" That smile reveals two well-established teeth on the bottom and one coming in on the top. He is clearly well prepared to enter nine months in November.

Max Observes:

- Okay, so I can clap hands. Terrific. On TV, a seal does it and gets something good to eat. When does that happen?
- I barely fit on the changing table now. Let's pay attention, please.
- The quote KID-TV shows unquote move much too fast and are way too loud. They drive me crazy. I do like the show where a lot of people run around with one ball and try to take it from each other. How come all of them have only one ball and I have dozens?

Max's Eighth Poem

I know I'm running out of time,
I see it in their faces,
The love is barely visible
The joy, not even traces.
I just can't sleep from ten to six,
I swear I really try,
And there's nothing else for me to do
But cry and cry and cry.
I could shut up and lie there
Which I guess would be most kind,
But eight hours without crying
Would destroy my little mind.
So come up with an answer
I don't want to be a creep,
You found a way to have me
Find a way to make me sleep.

Max
at Nine
Months

[He Crawls!]

Yes, at nine months Max began crawling. I realize there are many children who crawl earlier in their life but so what. Max didn't crawl until now because he was brought up on his back. He was never laid down on his stomach or allowed to sleep on his stomach to avoid suffocation. As a result, he was not used to pushing himself up to see what was going on. By lying on his back he saw everything, which accounts for his advanced intelligence and awareness over early crawlers. It is amazing that once he started crawling forward he mastered it quickly, making turns when necessary. He did, at first, crawl backward, something very few people have ever seen, and thereby earned the right to have that crawl named after him. He was doing "The Max." Make no mistake, crawling backwards is not silly.

It allows more time to reconsider the possible dangers that lie ahead. If there are none, there is no harm done other than knocking down the Lego construction that stands behind him, something easily corrected by his mother. He still does not like to eat in his high chair, or at all for that matter, although he seems to like yogurt and will accept it whenever or wherever it is offered to him.

Max has arrived at the point where his aging is so rapidly progressive that it has given rise to consideration of my own mortality. At sixty-six, I have to think of the "Will-I-be-around-fors." Let us quickly dispense with the obvious. I will not be around for his swearing in ceremony as President of the United States; that is at minimum 34-plus years from now which would make me one hundred years old so I think the 2033 inaugural ball is out of the question. Nor do I believe I will be around for his college, or medical school graduation, nor am I going to buy him presents for those events in advance. There has to be something to soften the blow. I sincerely am not disturbed by the thought that I will not be present for those wonderful moments in his life, nor disappointed that I will never know exactly what profession he enters, and for that matter whom he marries and how many children he will have. If I see him to be a wonderful child at five, I'll know he'll have a wonderful life, and if he's a rotten five-year-old kid, I won't want to see him when he's six. There's some chance that I will be around for his high school graduation. While sixteen years from now does not seem far away, the age of 83 does seem truly unattainable. I will of course do my best to make it mainly because I don't want to ruin his day by everybody walking around sadly saying, "It's such a shame his grandfather couldn't have lived to see this. He would really be smiling that great smile of theirs."

Max Observes:

- Now that I'm crawling can't you carpet the kitchen?
- Grampa was kidding about the electronic collar, wasn't he?
- No more visitors when I'm taking a bath, please.

Max's Ninth Poem

How come I have no "Grandma" like every
   other kid?
There's "MomMom" and there's "Bubbe"
Is it something that I did?
Well once I start my talking
I'll call them what I like
And "Bubbe" will be Bobo
And "MomMom" will be Mike.

Max
at Ten
Months

[Nobody's Perfect?]

Max and I went to a ski resort over the holiday season to sleigh ride and play cards. We included his mother and father, his grandmother and uncle and two cousins. He didn't want to eat, sleep or put on his snowsuit in 20 degree weather. Were he not such a charming kid otherwise, he would have been shipped home. However, he does have a bag of tricks now that makes him worth much of his complaining. In addition to clapping and raising his arms in response to the question, "How big is Max?", he now responds to the phrase "Bye Bye" with repeated clutching of his left hand. He also gives a high five and shakes his head "no" when his father shakes his head "no." He has also shown voluntary activity that indicates he is thinking. He turns his head away from incoming food while swatting it away with either hand. He can now stand, sit, crawl and roll onto his back or front at will. He can stand without support until he finds out he's doing it. And then there is his laughter. I am a comedy writer and over the past 40 years of my life I must have heard at least one million people laugh, none of whom laugh as perfectly as Max. As far as his refusal to eat, I don't know if I can blame him entirely. He is still on a sugar-free diet which makes for a lot of unappetizing jars. I did taste some of his food and it's not fun. What he does have, and it saved the vacation, is that wonderful Turteltaub smile that he continues to flash no matter what. He can be crying, grumbling or droning, but when he sees a friendly face, he throws in that amazing smile that now reveals four teeth, two on the bottom in close proximity to each other and two on the top separated by an inch and a half. I think there is another tooth that will appear between them or else we're talking thousands of dollars of orthodontia.

Max Observes:

- Sleepless or Eatless in Sun Valley is not my fault. It's the altitude. I came from Los Angeles, where the altitude is one hundred above zero to Sun Valley where it's six thousand square feet.

That's got to affect a kid who has no altitude at all. So give me a break.

- There's a kid in the park who keeps hitting me with his ball. Get his name and save it for me.
- Get rid of those intercoms between my room and yours. If you don't hear me, you'll sleep through and maybe I'll get tired of crying. Frankly, I'm fed up with this whole sleep thing.
- I should start walking in a few weeks but I don't see a helmet, knee pads or wrist pads around the house. Is it a question of money?

Max's Tenth Poem

It's been a bad month,
I had a virus, I had a cold,
A lot of stress,
At ten months old.
It's not my fault that I got sick
So mom and dad, get on the stick.

Max

at Eleven
Months

[Is That Walking?]

I have no doubt that by the end of this month, before Max is officially one year old, he will be walking. But this thing he is doing now at eleven-and-a-half is not walking. It is stumbling. Stumbling, it must be understood, is not a failure of any kind but a great advancement, and he does it very cutely. Being pointed by one parent toward another, and released, and moving his feet quickly to keep from falling and then being caught by the target parent, is plain and simple stumbling, not walking. Walking is being able to stop as well as go. In addition to stumbling, another skill he has mastered is pointing in the direction he wishes to be carried, and he has added the wonderful trick of placing his hand against his forehead in response to the question, "Do you have troubles?"

He still doesn't seem to enjoy being fed in his high chair, although if you walk over to him, wherever he may be playing or crawling, with a piece of bread, cheese or chicken, and put it near his mouth, he will eat it without objection. Sort of the reverse system of the drive-up window. He still smiles easily and often but I don't think he giggles as much as he did when he was a kid. I am not unwilling to take some of the blame for that. I realize it is possible that my offerings of humor are stale or not mature enough for him.

Physically, he is clearly growing up as he looks different each visit – and those visits are not more than a week apart. His front four teeth are fully visible and his hair is very blond now. When combed with a part he looks close to fifteen months old. Mainly, he simply is a very nice kid. And handsome besides cute. Great smile. I must add that his parents have done a wonderful job raising him. They shower him with love and intelligent concern. "As they were raised, so shall they raise."

Max Observes:

- So when I walk, where will I go? You have gates on the steps now. What happens when I can climb over them? Barbed wire?

- What are you keeping the fish in the tank for? You got the wrong guy if you think I'm going to eat them.
- I want to drive the car.

Max's Eleventh Poem

It's February, I know that word,
One of the first words that I
    ever heard.
Along with "inches," "pounds" and "cry,"
And "eighteenth." Did a year go by?
So many words I've yet to learn,
But what seems to be a shame,
The one that will be toughest
Is my own last name.
Tur...Truh...turlet...turder....

Max
at One
Year
Old

[Happy Birthday]

It is hard to believe that it was a full year ago that Adam called us in New York at 2 A.M. to tell us that Rhea was going to the hospital to have Max. It is equally hard to believe that we made airline reservations for an eight o'clock plane, flew to Los Angeles, arrived at 11:30 L.A. time and waited another two hours before Max was born. That was an exciting day in our lives and one filled with so many of God's blessings. We survived the plane flight, Rhea and Max survived the birth and both were, and remain, healthy. In the year since, we have seen baby and parents grow beautifully. Rhea and Adam are wonderful, loving, caring, sharing parents, who have made their son a happy and a healthy boy and put Shirley and me totally at ease about his living with them and not us. In his last few days leading to this birthday, he did walk real walking.

While he did not talk in the usual sense of the word, he has for several months communicated with sounds that clearly indicate "yes" and "no." Without saying "Mommy" or "Daddy" he knows to look toward each of them when their name is mentioned.

Above all, in one year he has developed a clear personality of good naturedness, intelligence, friendliness, charm and a sense of humor, proving that a kid can look like one grandfather and be like the other!

Max Observes:

- Just because I don't talk doesn't mean I have nothing to say. Stand by.
- Can I go right to skating? It looks easier than walking.
- I'm telling you right now, I'm not going to wear that Barney costume for any Halloween.
- How come it takes Mommy and Daddy so long to kiss each other? When they kiss me it's over in a second.
- I love my family!!!

Max's Twelfth Poem

I'd like to thank my Mom and Dad,
You stuck with me through good and bad,
And got me to the age of one,
But don't go 'way 'cause I'm not done...
I need swimming lessons!!!

Afterword

[Notes, Games & Quotes]

Yesterday, a friend asked me how I felt about "having a grandson to continue the name." I had never thought about that. Now having done so, I realize it matters to me for my father. I believe it would have been important to him although not so much to me. I think he would have been pleased to know the name Turteltaub would go on for many generations as it will if Maxie has a son. My father, Bernard, was the first Turteltaub to become special. He overcame polio as a three year old to become a successful businessman and community leader, gathering some fame in the northern New Jersey area as a candidate for Mayor of Englewood, a newspaper columnist during World War II and County Chairman of the March of Dimes. As a first generation American, he was proud of himself and his accomplishments and therefore prouder of his name, and I believe rightfully so, than was any of his progeny.

He would have liked that name to go on, and so I am glad it will. I hesitate to feel pride for myself because I sincerely believe it is unfair for the name to go on and reflect only the Turteltaub side of the family and not the Steinberg side. My wife and her family are entitled to as much honor for future deeds accomplished by our sons, grandsons and great grandsons. I know that Max, being the kind of kid he is, would agree with me.

First Year Games
(For the grandfather who wants to get it right)

I. PEEKABOO*
Number of players: Two. One Child, one Adult.

EQUIPMENT:
One of the following: Blanket, handkerchief, door, doorway, couch, chair, hallway, building – to name the most popular.

---

*Peekaboo is not the same as "Peekaboo, I see You."

Peekaboo is simply Peek and Boo. You hide, peek at your grandchild and when he spots you, you say "Boo." Saying "Boo" is more startling than saying "I see you," which is usually said more sweetly and cutely than "Boo," and is therefore more a grandmother's game. Whereas "I see you" will evoke a smile from the baby at best, "Boo" will often get a laugh.

The best way to say "Boo" when the time comes is to put your lips together, open your eyelids as wide as they can go and jerkily thrust your head forward as you say it.

PLAYING THE GAME: The object is to get a laugh from your grandchild by suddenly appearing before him from behind a blind and shouting "boo" at him. (Shouting or saying "Peekaboo" has become acceptable.)

The blind may be anything that comes between you and your grandchild. It may either hide you until you reveal yourself, or hide the grandchild until you pull it away to reveal him or her. A popular piece of equipment is the diaper–clean. You put it over your face, pull it away and shout "Boo," or put it over the baby's face and pull it away and so on.

POPULAR VARIATION: Try this, this is fun: While out of sight of the baby, first say, "Where is Grampa, PopPop?" or whatever name you go by.

Another variation that has gained popularity in recent years is to eliminate shouting "Peekaboo" or "Boo," but responding to your own question, "Where is Grampa?" with "Here he is!" as you reveal yourself.

This innovation clearly inspired the matching variation of asking "Where is the baby?" when the baby is hidden, and answering with "There he or she is!" when the diaper, blanket or lamp shade is pulled off of his or her head.

II. WHERE'S YOUR NOSE?

This is a game that isn't played intelligently until the fifth or sixth month. It is identical to the games: Where's Your Mouth?, Where's Your Eyes? and Where's Your Ears? While it is grammatically correct to say "Where Are Your Eyes" and "...Your Ears," it is unnecessary to do so.

Number of Players: Two

EQUIPMENT:
One Nose.

The game starts early on in the child's career by the grandfather touching the baby's nose and repeating, "Here's your nose." Several months later, when the child has acquired memory patterns, the grandfather then says to the baby, "Where's Your Nose?" and the baby makes an attempt at hitting or touching it.

THE VARIATION: After the baby has some idea of what "Nose" is, the grandfather may try, "Where's Grampa's Nose?" leaning in as close as possible to the baby. In time the baby will hit him on it.

For some real fun, when the baby hits your nose, go "Beep!" He will soon hit your nose to hear you go "Beep" without you asking, "Where's Grampa's nose?"

III. THIS LITTLE PIGGY WENT TO MARKET
Number of Players: Two

EQUIPMENT:
Five toes or fingers which, for the purpose of this game, are called "Piggies."

Before playing, the grandfather should memorize the following free verse:

This little piggy went to market.
This little piggy stayed home.
This little piggy had roast beef.
This little piggy had none.
And this little piggy went wheeeeeeeeeee all the
way home.

Assuming we are playing with the grandchild's toes rather than fingers, the grandfather takes the baby's bare foot in one hand, holding it firmly but carefully, and with his thumb and forefinger of his other hand gently squeezes the small toe and says:

This little piggy went to market.
(He then takes the next toe and says):
This little piggy stayed home.
(Pinching the next toe he goes on):
This little piggy had roast beef.
(And regarding the fourth toe):
This little piggy had none.

And finally, to the baby's surprise the first time this is done and with great anticipation each time thereafter, still holding the baby's foot securely, the grandfather barely squeezes the large toe and declares:

And this little piggy went wheeeeeeeeeee all the way home.

The excitement comes from the grandfather letting go of the big toe quickly and tickling the baby all the way up his leg to his neck, commencing with the word, wheeeeeeeeeee.

To play this with the baby's fingers instead of the toes, substitute fingers accordingly, keeping the same rhyme and rhythm.

Max's Addendum Observation:

I'm not really wild about those games but Grampa loves them. It must be that grandfather thing.

Looking Back

Since this book was completed on Max's first birthday, two years have passed. In that time:

Max outgrew all the clothes he was going to grow into, his crib and his high chair.

Bubbe canceled two vacation trips to Europe to be around in case she was needed to babysit.

Max mastered the English language, including his last name.

I learned the names of all the friends of Thomas the Tank Engine, as well as the station master, Mr. Toppemhattem.

Max mastered the computer, Elmo-wise.

PopPop, the other grandfather, entered his and Max's pictures in a grandfather-grandson look-alike contest and won.

I stopped talking to PopPop.

Max received one write-in vote in the historic presidential election of 2000. (All right, so call it "The Grandfather Thing.")

Famous Grandfather Quotations

The reason grandparents and grandchildren get along so well is they share a common enemy...the parents.

—Anonymous

Grandchildren don't make a man feel old. It's the knowledge that he's married to a grandmother.

—G. Norman Collie

Our children are here to stay, but our babies and toddlers and preschoolers are gone as fast as they grow up–and we have only a short moment with each. When you see a grandfather take a baby in his arms, you see that the moment hasn't always been long enough.

—St. Clair Adams Sullivan

Grandchildren are the only justification we have for not having killed our kids.

—Nancy Spence

There is no woman more precious than the daughter who will not allow her father to change her child's diaper.

—Saul Turteltaub

How confusing the beams from memory's lamps are, one day a bachelor, the next a Grampa. What is the secret of the trick? How did I get so old so quick?

—Ogden Nash
Preface to the past, 1957

Greatness of name in the father often times overwhelms the son. They stand too near one another, the shadow kills the growth; so much, that we see the grandchild come more and oftener to be heir of the first.

—Ben Johnson